D0065470

The Illustrated Book of
MINDFUL
MEDITATIONS
for MINDLESS
MOMENTS

The Illustrated Book of
MINDFUL MEDITATIONS

for MINDLESS MOMENTS

COURTNEY E. ACKERMAN

Adams Media
New York • London • Toronto • Sydney • New Delhi

Aadamsmedia

Adams Media
An Imprint of Simon & Schuster, Inc.
57 Littlefield Street
Avon, Massachusetts 02322

First Adams Media hardcover edition December 2020

ADAMS MEDIA and colophon are trademarks of Simon & Schuster.

For information about special discounts for bulk purchases, please contact Simon & Schuster Special Sales at 1-866-506-1949 or business@ simonandschuster.com.

The Simon & Schuster Speakers Bureau can bring authors to your live event. For more information or to book an event contact the Simon & Schuster Speakers Bureau at 1-866-248-3049 or visit our website at www.simonspeakers.com.

Interior design by Sylvia McArdle
Interior illustrations by Priscilla Yuen

Manufactured in China

10 9 8 7 6 5 4 3 2 1

Library of Congress Cataloging-in-Publication Data has been applied for.

ISBN 978-1-5072-1437-4
ISBN 978-1-5072-1438-1 (ebook)

DEDICATION

No dedication would be complete without mentioning my wonderful family and friends who offer me love, support, and kindness day in and day out, but this book is truly dedicated to all the lovely people who pick it up and give these exercises a try. You're all amazing!

ACKNOWLEDGMENTS

A big, heartfelt thank-you goes out to all the people who helped get this book off the ground.

Thank you to Jackie Musser and Julia Jacques, my editors extraordinaire!

Thank you to Katie Corcoran Lytle for helping me refine and improve.

Thank you to the publisher, illustrator, and everyone else involved in the process of getting this book finished, printed, and out on the shelves.

Finally, a big thank-you to my family and friends for supporting and inspiring me. I love you all.

CONTENTS

INTRODUCTION

Brushing your teeth? Filling up your gas tank? Cooking dinner? These may sound like run-of-the-mill, everyday tasks, but they're actually incredible opportunities to practice meditation.

You've probably heard of the many wonderful benefits of meditation—a clearer head, more inner peace, and a greater sense of gratitude—but you might be having trouble integrating it into your life, or maybe you don't even know how to get started! Fortunately, the quick and easy meditations throughout *The Illustrated Book of Mindful Meditations for Mindless Moments* will show you that you *do* have time to meditate. And, contrary to what you might have heard, you don't need to dedicate a big block of time to sitting cross-legged in absolute silence to reap the benefits. All you need to do is practice mindfulness during the everyday activities that you're already going to be doing anyway!

Mindfulness is all about paying attention to what's happening around you and being aware of yourself and your environment—and it's the key to quieting your mind for the illustrated everyday meditations throughout the book. So pay attention when you feel the water running over your skin in the shower. Realize how good it feels when you cross something off your to-do list at work. Notice the different textures of your clothes when you fold your laundry. And realize that, when you're mindful, the little things in life don't have to be so little.

MEDITATION AT HOME

Making your favorite morning beverage. Vacuuming. Pulling weeds. In this part you'll learn how to turn these normal everyday activities into mindful meditations that you can do around the house. After all, if you can be mindful at home, you can be mindful anywhere!

BRUSHING YOUR TEETH

Be mindful as you apply toothpaste to your toothbrush. Note the intense, minty flavor as you brush. Feel each sensation as you move the brush over your gums, your tongue, and your teeth. Enjoy the clean feeling.

WASHING YOUR FACE

Feel the sensation of the water splashing on your face and hands. Notice the smell of the soap and the way it moves over your skin. Enjoy the feeling of being clean and refreshed.

TAKING
A SHOWER

As you step into the shower, take note of the water hitting your skin. Feel its warmth. Smell your shampoo as you pour it into your hands and lather up, and enjoy the luxurious feel as you work it into your hair.

GETTING DRESSED

Choose your clothing in the morning with care. Consider how it moves against your fingers. Note how it feels to slip it on over your head or pull it up your legs.

MAKING COFFEE OR TEA

As you prepare your morning drink, stay focused on the steps involved. Smell the coffee or tea as you put it into the machine or teapot. Listen to the drip of the coffee. Watch the steam rise from your tea. Then give your full attention to the taste of your drink as you take your first sip.

VACUUMING THE HOUSE

Move the vacuum across the carpet. Notice how your hand and arm feel as you push and pull the machine. Take note of the vacuum's route as it passes over the floor, leaving a clean pathway behind it.

TAKING OUT THE TRASH

Gather your trash and get it ready to go. Take a moment to feel the smooth material of the bag under your fingertips. As you walk to the trash can or garbage chute, be mindful of your steps and the weight of the bag swinging by your side.

PAYING
YOUR BILLS

Whether you sign in online or write out a check, notice the movements your hands and arms make as you pay your bills. Feel the smoothness of the pen in your hand or the keys on your keyboard.

FOLDING LAUNDRY

Identify each item as you take it out of the dryer. Fold each item as efficiently as you can. Breathe in the smell of warm, clean laundry.

WATERING THE GARDEN

Feel the weight of the hose in your hand. Make note of the change in pressure as you turn the water on. Watch the water as it sprinkles over your plants, and think about how it helps them grow.

PULLING WEEDS

Feel the leaves of the weeds under your fingers or the texture of your gloves. Look up to see the sun or the clouds in the sky. Close your eyes and sense the breeze. Smell the fresh air.

CHECKING THE MAIL

Walk mindfully to your mailbox, paying attention to your surroundings. Open the box, taking care to feel the metal with your fingertips. Note how the box's lid swings on its hinges. Take your mail and feel the smooth paper in your hands.

ORGANIZING YOUR JUNK DRAWER

As you take each item out of your junk drawer, consider how it feels in your hand. Think about how the item is used. Put it in its proper place and enjoy the new organization.

CLEANING OUT YOUR BAG

As you open your bag, take note of each thing you can see. Consider each object as you encounter it, and think about why you have it. If you don't need it, say goodbye to it!

ADJUSTING THE TEMPERATURE

Feel the coolness or the warmth in the air as you go to adjust the temperature. Feel the pressure on your fingertips as you press the button or shift the indicator, and listen as the furnace or air conditioner turns on or off.

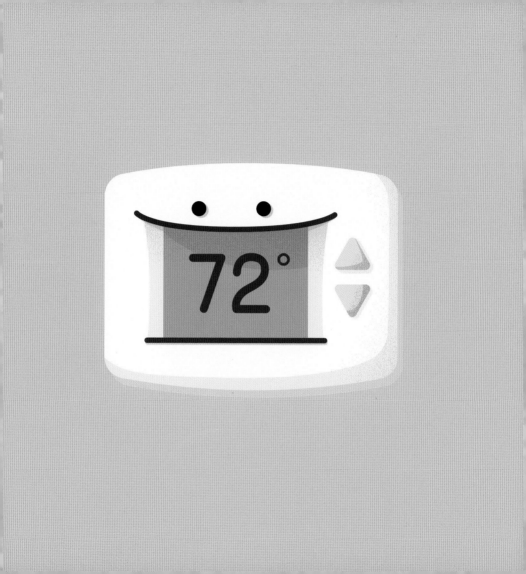

COOKING DINNER

As you prepare your ingredients, pay attention to how each one feels and smells. Listen to the sound of each ingredient hitting the pan and watch the steam rise.

WIPING DOWN THE TABLE

Clear all the remnants of your meal from the table. Grab a sponge or dish towel and swipe it slowly across the table, noting each crumb and bit of food as it is swept away. Admire the clean surface once you're done.

LOCKING
THE DOOR

As you lock the door for the night, move slowly. Grip the lock tightly and feel the smooth, cool metal. Turn it and notice when it clicks into place.

TURNING ON
A LIGHT

Feel the light switch under your fingers as you flip it. Listen for a slight electrical hum as the bulb jumps to life. Watch as your surroundings light up.

EMPTYING THE DISHWASHER

Notice the heat and steam coming from your dishwasher when you open the door. Admire the cleanliness of the dishes as you put them away. Feel the smoothness of your plates and utensils, and take note of the weight of each item as you find its proper place.

PUTTING ON PAJAMAS

Feel the comfortable fabric of your pajamas. Notice how your body relaxes when you put them on. Enjoy the feeling of being ready to rest after a long and busy day.

GETTING INTO BED

As you pull back the covers, take a minute to look at your bed, ready for you to slide in. Think about how comfy and cozy your bed looks. Feel the smoothness of your sheets as you climb in and pull them up over you.

MEDITATION ON THE GO

Whether you're hopping in the car, heading to an appointment, or looking over the produce at the grocery store, you can find moments to cultivate mindfulness. It's easier to stay mindful when you're somewhere quiet and comfortable, but your ability to be mindful in busy, loud, and unfamiliar places will serve you well. Practice meditating on the go to take your skills to the next level.

HEADING OUT THE DOOR

Take a moment to look at your front door as you close and lock it. See the color; notice if there are any chips in the paint. Turn around and look at the view from your front door for a moment, and then set off on your way.

TAKING PUBLIC TRANSPORTATION

Once you're settled in, take advantage of the opportunity to sit and look out the window as someone else does the driving. Watch the scenery go by. Pay attention to how the bus or train moves along its route.

TURNING ON YOUR CAR

Take the keys and slide them slowly into the ignition. Feel the engine start up as you turn the key. Listen to the sound of the car running before you put it in gear and drive away.

WAITING IN LINE

Look at the people ahead of you in line and note their posture. See if it says anything to you about their mood or their patience level. Think about your own posture and how it makes your body feel.

WALKING AROUND TOWN

As you walk from one place to the next, think about putting one foot in front of the other. Look at your surroundings as you walk by shops, houses, storefronts, and parks. Listen to the noises around you.

SITTING AT A RED LIGHT

Once your car stops, take your hands off the wheel and mindfully stretch out your fingers. Hear the noises of the cars driving past. Notice the other cars stopped at the light and see what the drivers are doing.

HOLDING THE DOOR FOR SOMEONE

As you walk into a store or other business, be aware of other people walking in or out. Push against the weight of the door as you hold it open for them and feel the release of that weight once they've passed.

SHOPPING

When you find the items on your shopping list, be mindful of how each item feels as you grab it and put it in your cart. Notice how the shopping cart takes a little more effort to push as you fill it.

PAYING FOR GROCERIES

When you go to pay for your groceries, notice the last-minute products that surround you. Watch the smooth progress of your items as the conveyor belt moves them to the cashier. Read the name on your cashier's name tag.

ORDERING A MEAL

Think about the ingredients included in each dish as you read through the menu. Consider how well they go together, then picture each item and how it would taste.

CHECKING YOUR REFLECTION

As you pass a mirror or window, pause to look at your reflection. See yourself as you are in the current moment. Notice what you're wearing, how your hair looks, and what your expression is like. Smile at yourself.

LISTENING TO YOUR FAVORITE SONG

When your favorite song comes on, take a moment to pause and really listen to the lyrics and the message the song puts forward. Notice the different sounds and instruments that make up the song. Think about how it makes you feel.

PEOPLE-WATCHING

Pick a bench or sit in your car for a few moments and watch the people who pass by. Look at their faces, notice what they are wearing, and see what they are doing as they walk. Consider what they are feeling as they pass by.

WORKING OUT

Look at your workout equipment—whether it's weights, a yoga mat, or a treadmill—and think about which part of your body it exercises. Focus on each repetition as you lift weights, or each breath as you get your cardio in. Notice how your body feels in the moment.

FILLING UP YOUR GAS TANK

When you're pumping gas, feel the smooth handle of the gas nozzle under your fingers. Notice the flow of the gas when you pull the lever and your gas tank begins to fill. Smell the gas in the air as you put the nozzle back on the pump.

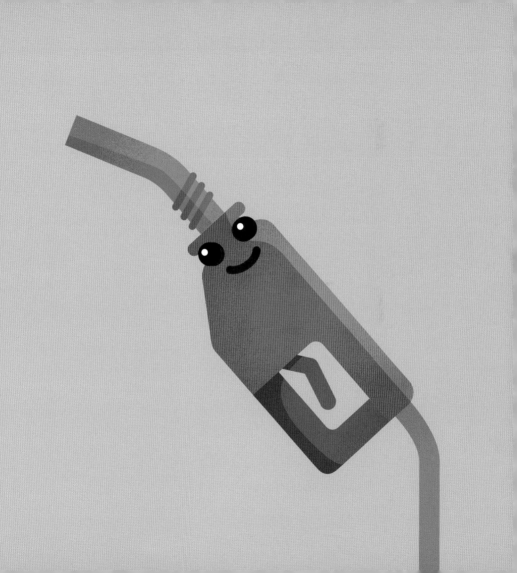

GRABBING COFFEE

See the busy baristas making drinks, smell all the different coffees and teas as they brew, and hear the clangs and clacks and beeps as the machinery does its job. Feel the temperature of the cup in your hand as you pick up your order.

CHECKING YOUR SOCIAL MEDIA

Think about what you're expecting to see as your app loads. Watch as new content replaces the old as you scroll through. Feel the smooth glass of your phone as you swipe up and down.

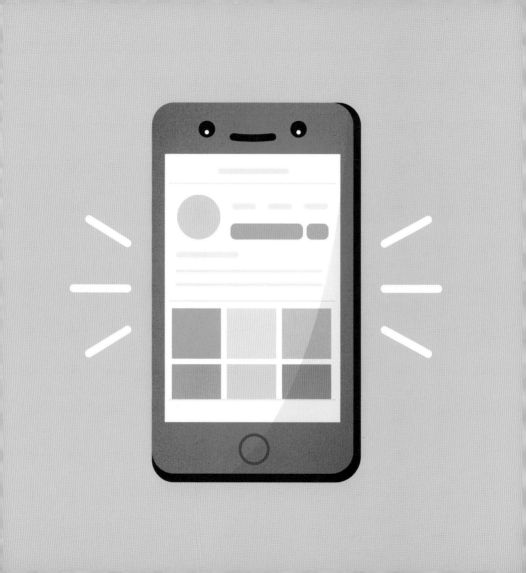

CHEWING GUM

Taste the minty or fruity flavor of your gum. Roll the gum around with your tongue, chew it, and blow a bubble, paying attention to how your mouth feels as you do each of these things.

CHECKING THE TIME

Before you check the time, pause to ask yourself about what time it feels like. Compare your guess to see if you were right. If you were off, think about what made it feel like a different time to you.

GETTING HOME

As you pull into your driveway or open your front door after a long day of work, errands, or chores, notice how it feels to get home. Note the smells and sounds as you walk in the door. Ask yourself if anything looks different from when you left this morning.

MEDITATION AT WORK

The humdrum routine of the office provides an excellent environment for working in some everyday meditation. If you look closely, you'll find tons of opportunities to be extra mindful. Look for space where you can squeeze in meditation while you're doing activities like writing an email, waiting for a meeting to start, or organizing your documents. Just a little extra mindfulness in the office (or wherever you work) can boost your well-being and your productivity at the same time!

WALKING INTO WORK

Look around you as you walk into work. See the building, the parking lot, the door, and the lobby or entryway. Notice what is beautiful or interesting. Pay attention to how walking in makes you feel.

GETTING SETTLED IN

As you settle in for your workday, take note of the things you see around your workspace. Take a guess as to whether you will use each item or not, based on what you have to do today.

FIRING UP THE COMPUTER

Take a moment to observe your computer as you turn it on and watch the screen come to life. See the clear, bright screen and feel the smoothness of the keys on the keyboard.

CHECKING YOUR CALENDAR

Note all of your meetings and appointments for the day as you check your calendar. Think about where each will take place, who you will meet with, and what you need to prepare for each meeting.

WRITING AN EMAIL

Think about the words you choose as you write. Feel the keys as you purposefully press each one and watch as the letters appear on the screen. Consider your intentions and whether your wording matches them before you hit Send.

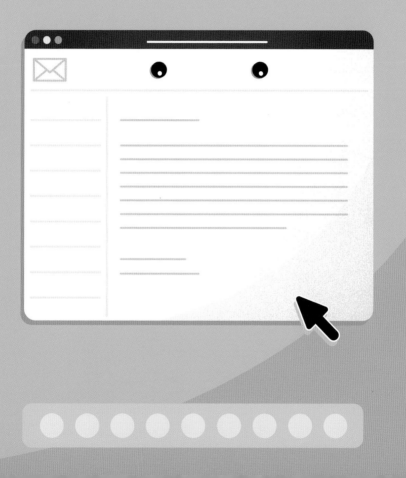

TAKING A BREAK

Put your "away message" on, relax your body, and take a deep breath. Close your eyes and pay attention to the sounds around you. Separate out each individual sound and notice where it's coming from (the printer, a telephone ringing, etc.).

LOOKING OUT THE WINDOW

Look out the window and take note of what you see. Count the birds or the telephone poles. Look at the trees or hanging flags and decide whether it's windy or not.

WAITING ON HOLD

When you are waiting on hold, listen mindfully. If there is music, see if you can note the instruments used. If it's a quiet line, see if you can hear anything else, like a slight hum or a buzz.

SITTING AT YOUR DESK

As you sit, take a moment to arrange your body so your back is flush against the chair and your feet are flat on the floor. Note how each part of your body feels in your desk chair, from your head down to your feet.

CROSSING A TASK OFF YOUR TO-DO LIST

Revel in the sense of accomplishment as you cross off a task, even if it's small. Feel the movement of the pen as you draw a decisive line through the task, and then mentally cross it out in your head too. Take a moment to celebrate before moving to the next task.

STOPPING AT A COWORKER'S DESK

When you stop to check in with a coworker, notice how their desk or office is arranged. Pay attention to the personal items that they've brought in from home. What does their space tell you about them?

WAITING FOR A MEETING TO START

When you're waiting for your meeting to start, take a look around and note who is in the meeting. Feel the seat beneath you and see your notes on the conference table. Prepare to listen mindfully once the meeting begins.

LISTENING TO CHATTER

As your coworkers chat nearby, take a minute to listen. Don't eavesdrop, but take note of the tone of the conversation. Hear the rise and fall of their voices as the discussion continues.

SIGNING AN OFFICE CARD

As you take the office folder and pull out the card you need to sign, take a moment to think about the person you're celebrating. Note the pattern of the blank spaces on the card. See the different handwriting and pen colors used by your coworkers.

GETTING SOME WATER

Head down to the watercooler and make note of what you see on the way. Listen to the glugging noise the water makes as it filters out. Watch as your bottle or cup slowly fills to the brim.

ORGANIZING YOUR DOCUMENTS

As you shuffle your papers around, notice how the paper feels on your fingertips. Lift the papers in your hands and feel their weight. Guess how many pages there are. Think about the different ways to organize your notes.

WALKING DOWN THE HALLWAY

As you walk down the hallway, look up, down, and around you. Notice the carpet or flooring under your feet. See the color of the walls and the lights overhead. See what you don't usually see.

GREETING A CUSTOMER OR CLIENT

When a customer or client walks in, take a quick moment to clear your mind and greet them with your full attention. Make eye contact, give them a meaningful hello, and listen attentively to what they have to say.

EATING LUNCH

Whether you sit in your office's breakroom, a cafeteria, or at your desk, take a second to note the aroma of your meal. Take a small bite; taste all the different flavors and feel the food in your mouth. Savor each bite.

DOODLING ON YOUR NOTEPAD

Take a short mental break and doodle on your notepad. Draw anything that comes to mind. See how it feels to put pen to paper with no goal in mind.

SQUEEZING A STRESS BALL

Feel the weight of the stress ball in your hand. Squeeze it lightly and notice how squishy it is. Give it a hard squeeze and note its resistance to being crushed. Pay attention to how the ball feels as it springs back into shape.

HAVING AN AFTERNOON SNACK

As you choose your afternoon snack, think about how it will taste. When you take a bite, notice the sensations as the food travels down your throat and into your stomach. Consider whether it tastes as good as you thought it would.

STRETCHING OUT

Stand up, reach your hands up overhead, and point your toes, stretching from top to bottom. Consider how the stretch feels in each part of your body. Then notice how your whole body feels when the stretch is released.

HEADING HOME FOR THE DAY

Pay attention to your routine as you get ready to head home at the end of your workday. Note how it feels when you switch off your computer, push your chair in toward your desk, and grab your bag. Release yourself from the pressures of the day as you walk out the door.

MEDITATION WITH LOVED ONES

You might wonder how you could meditate with others around, but it's actually a perfect time to transform an everyday moment into something bigger. Spending time with your loved ones can put you in a more loving and kind mindset, which makes it easier to step into mindfulness. In this part you'll learn how to cultivate mindfulness while asking about someone's day, giving a hug, and even while watching TV with a friend or family member.

GREETING
A FRIEND

As you greet a friend, notice how your mood changes for the better. Enjoy the happy feeling that comes over you and show your joy with a smile.

ASKING ABOUT SOMEONE'S DAY

Check in with a loved one about their day and stay present as they respond. Truly listen to their answer, offer them an appropriate response, and connect with them.

PLAYING A GAME WITH A LOVED ONE

When you're not actively playing the game, take a moment to sit in stillness. See each of the game pieces on the board or feel the slippery cards in your hands. Think about how nice it feels to take a break and do something fun with someone you love.

SHARING A MEAL

As you eat with someone you love, savor both the food and the friend. Pay attention to the food's tastes, smells, and sounds. Note what dishes your friend enjoys the most.

TAKING A WALK TOGETHER

As you walk with your friend, point out things you notice and ask them what they see and hear. Stay in step with your loved one and feel the natural rhythm of your footsteps as you walk in sync.

CALLING
A FRIEND

As you pull up your friend's contact info in your phone, take a second to visualize them. Imagine what they're doing right now and what they'll say when they pick up.

MEETING FOR BRUNCH

When you pull up to the restaurant to meet a friend, pay attention to how you feel (excited to see your friend, looking forward to the meal, etc.). Keep these feelings present as you make your way inside to meet them.

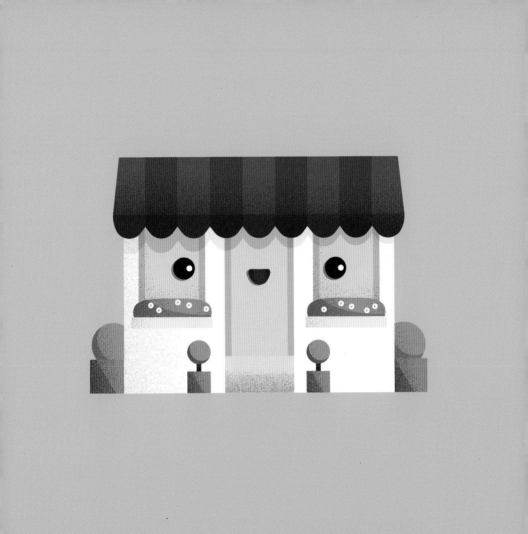

SMILING AT A STRANGER

Look for a friendly face around you and make eye contact. Share your joy with a purposeful smile, send them a bit of your good energy, then move on with your day.

GIVING A HUG

Let yourself melt into the hug and stay there for as long as you need. Feel the love and care as you hold your loved one. Note the warmth you get from their embrace.

HOLDING SOMEONE'S HAND

As you hold your loved one's hand, stay open to their kindness. Notice the feel of their skin. Savor the warm, happy feeling you get from their touch.

LAUGHING TOGETHER

Whatever the source of the laughter, stay present as you enjoy a laugh with a loved one. Open yourself up to the joy of laughing together and let your loved one's giggles fuel even more of your own.

LOOKING AT A LOVED ONE

When you have a moment, take a mindful look at someone you love. See them through the eyes of love, care, and compassion. Note all the things you love about them.

SHARING EYE CONTACT

If you have a loved one who is open to this, try making eye contact with them. Look deeply into their eyes and be present and open. Observe the colors and flecks in their eyes. Try to read their feelings.

SAYING
THANK YOU

When someone does a good deed or kind act for you, say a mindful thank you. Keep the good deed in mind and express your gratitude. Imagine the care your loved one took to help you, and repay it with sincerity.

WATCHING TV TOGETHER

Sit in comfortable silence with a friend as you watch TV together. Notice how the couch or chair feels underneath you. See how your friend reacts to the show you're watching together. Be mindful of how nice it is to simply sit and relax in the presence of a loved one.

CHECKING YOUR PHONE

If you find yourself checking your phone when you're with a loved one, be aware of the situation. If using your phone is not necessary, make the mindful decision to put it down, enjoy the moment, and focus your attention on your friend.

GOING
FOR A DRIVE

When you're in the passenger seat, take a moment to sit in silence and look out the car window. Watch as the pavement speeds by and objects blur. Take note of the scenery, whether it's a beautiful landscape or a busy city street.

LISTENING TO MUSIC WITH A FRIEND

When you're in the car with a friend, let them choose what you listen to. Listen to the rhythms, note the beat, and hear the words together. Be fully present with the music and with your loved one.

PARTING WAYS

Savor your last moment with your loved one. Note the small details about them that you'll miss the most, and then say goodbye. Look forward to seeing them again.

ABOUT THE AUTHOR

Courtney E. Ackerman is the author of *My Pocket Positivity*, *5-Minute Bliss*, *My Pocket Gratitude*, and *My Pocket Meditations for Self-Compassion*. Her early travels sparked her interest in learning about human nature at a young age. This interest led her to Claremont Graduate University, where she earned her master's degree in positive psychology and program evaluation, studying compassion, survey research, and psychological assessments. She enjoys reading and writing, spending time with her dogs, and going to tastings at local breweries and wineries.